Discovering ART

Impressionism

Other titles in the *Discovering Art* series include:

Animation

Anime and Manga

Graphic Arts

Sculpture

Discovering ART

Impressionism

Kris Hirschmann

ReferencePoint
Press®

San Diego, CA

© 2015 ReferencePoint Press, Inc.
Printed in the United States

For more information, contact:
ReferencePoint Press, Inc.
PO Box 27779
San Diego, CA 92198
www.ReferencePointPress.com

LIBRARY OF CONGRESS CATALOGING-IN-PUBLICATION DATA

Hirschmann, Kris, 1967–
  Impressionism / by Kris Hirschmann.
    pages cm. — (Discovering art)
  Includes bibliographical references and index.
  ISBN-13: 978-1-60152-700-4 (hardback)
  ISBN-10: 1-60152-700-4 (hardback)
  1. Impressionism (Art)—Juvenile literature. I. Title.
  ND192.I4H57 2014
  759.05'4--dc23
                                                    2014014190

Contents

What Is Impressionist Art?

In April 1874 a group of independent painters opened an exhibition of their work in Paris, France. The art they displayed was very unusual for the era. Instead of subjects drawn from the Bible or classic mythology, as was typical at the time, these works portrayed landscapes and everyday scenes. Instead of the precise brushwork then considered essential, they included careless paint slashes and strokes. Instead of careful attention to detail, they displayed an artistic freedom that verged on the sloppy.

Most art critics were appalled at what they saw. They wrote scathing reviews of the show. These reviews were printed in the most important magazines and newspapers of the time. The art community was determined to let the public know that this new art was unacceptable. This, the experts said over and over, was *not* the way things were done.

One such expert was a critic named Louis Leroy. On April 25, 1874, Leroy published an article that poked fun at the exhibition. Part review and part satire, the piece was a dialogue between two imaginary visitors to the show. The visitors were merciless in their commentary, flinging insults at both the art and the artists who had created it. No one escaped the characters' clever but mean-spirited barbs.

Leroy's speakers were particularly critical of a work entitled *Impression: Sunrise* (1872). The painting showed the morning sun rising above a foggy harbor. Boats, buildings, smoke, and water were implied with a few scant brush strokes. The end result was a wash of color that gave the feeling of the moment without providing any real details. Standing in front of this work, one speaker uttered this scornful summary: "Impressionism—I was certain of it. I was just telling myself that, since I was impressed, there had to be some impression in it . . . and what freedom, what ease of workmanship! Wallpaper in its embryonic state is more finished than that seascape."[1]

Impressionism. The word was written in jest, and it was meant as an insult. Little did Leroy know that his made-up word would come to define the artists and the art form that he despised.

An Apt Term

It is not hard to see why Leroy's word caught on. The term *Impressionism* was an apt term for art that conveyed a feeling, an impression, rather than a precisely realistic image or a story. Claude Monet, the artist whose painting inspired the term, frankly admitted as much in an interview many years later. "I had sent a thing done in Le Havre, from my window, sun in the mist and a few masts of boats sticking up in the foreground. They asked me for a title for the catalogue, it couldn't really be taken for a view of Le Havre, and I said: 'Put *Impression*.'"[2]

Monet's words underscore the purpose of the Impressionist movement. The artists were not trying to record every detail of the scenes they painted. Rather, they were trying to capture fleeting moments in time. They were fascinated by the way different types of light, shadow, and colors interacted with objects, and their goal was to transfer these effects to canvas. They also wanted to capture the feelings or the moods that these effects

> **Words in Context**
> *Impressionism*
> A genre of art that seeks to capture an impression rather than to strictly represent objects and details.

Claude Monet's 1872 painting *Impression: Sunrise* (pictured) inspired the term *Impressionism* in describing a new style of art. This new art style, which favored landscapes and everyday scenes depicted through seemingly haphazard brush strokes, was not initially well received.

produced. Once an artist decided that a piece met these standards, the work was done, even if the painting might look unfinished to an observer.

The men and women now known as Impressionists were not the first artists to experiment with these techniques. They *were* the first, however, to devote themselves to this new artistic style. Some of the Impressionists dabbled in this mode for just a few years before moving on to new challenges. Others made Impressionism their lives' work. Either way, these artists collectively changed the course of art history. They rocked the art world's attitudes and methods in ways that persist to this day.

Twelve Years of Change

Despite its huge and long-lasting impact, what historians now call the French Impressionist movement was surprisingly limited in scope. It occurred almost exclusively in the region around Paris, France. It had a small group of adherents, most of whom had studied art together and who spent time together socially. It also emerged during a short but turbulent period. The first exhibition of the Impressionists occurred in 1874; the eighth and last exhibition occurred just twelve years later, in 1886.

Roughly thirty artists exhibited with the Impressionist group at one time or another. Not all of these artists, however, worked in the Impressionist style. Art historians agree that only a handful of people truly represent the Impressionist movement. The key participants include Claude Monet, Pierre-Auguste Renoir, Alfred Sisley, Frédéric Bazille, Berthe Morisot, and Mary Cassatt. Strongly associated with the group but holding fast to certain differences of style and theory were Camille Pissarro, Édouard Manet, and Edgar Degas.

These men and women, and other artists to varying degrees, are notable as much for their vision as their talent. They developed new methods of seeing and painting the world. By recording their impressions, these pioneers opened the door for future artists to do the same in other new and exciting ways.

Impressionism's Legacy

This impact was felt immediately. Encouraged by the success of the Impressionists, artists everywhere started experimenting with fresh ways to express themselves on canvas. Paul Cézanne, for example, became an expert at creating images by using large areas of color instead of strokes. Georges Seurat crafted massive paintings using nothing but tiny dots of pure color. Pablo Picasso and many others abandoned realism altogether in favor of blocky, abstract shapes.

The list does not stop there. Countless artists, both famous and obscure, have worked since the Impressionist era to develop new avenues of artistic expression. All of these artists seek to communicate something through their work, and in this sense, art historians say, all of today's art hails from the Impressionist era. Viewers may not always understand the messages buried in modern pieces, but they respect the artist's right to create whatever he or she likes. From realistic to abstract to everything in between, good art continues to make an impression.

Chapter One

Setting the Scene

The Impressionist movement began in the 1870s with a group of artists living in and around Paris, France. Most of these artists were young, and they were all talented and enthusiastic. They were eager to make a splash in the art world, and they wanted to do it on their own terms. In their youthful exuberance the budding Impressionists embraced techniques and topics that were frowned upon by society in general and the fine arts community in particular.

Given these facts, it is fair to say that the Impressionist movement was partly driven by the personalities of the artists involved. But this is only one small part of a much bigger picture. Impressionism was born during a time of incredible change and upheaval. This social tumult was an integral part of the life experiences and perspectives of the Impressionists. It shaped not only who they were but also, ultimately, the art they produced. To understand Impressionist art, therefore, it is important to understand the conditions from which it emerged.

State of the Arts

The foundations of the Paris art scene were laid a full two hundred years before Impressionism emerged. In 1667 the French king Louis XIV and his ministers created an organization called the Salon at the Palace of the Louvre. The Salon's job was to support art and artists that the French government approved. It did this by hosting massive exhibitions where artists could earn cash prizes and public exposure. Artists who were accepted into these shows enjoyed great popularity and success. Those who did not had nowhere else to show their work, so they remained poor and unknown.

At first the Salon had a very small stable of exhibitors. It allowed only a few artists to participate in its shows. But as time went by and the Salon's shows became more popular, the organization broadened its approach. By the early 1800s Salon exhibitions were open to artists of all nationalities and ages. Thousands of painters applied for admission.

These applications were scrutinized by a jury consisting of Salon members. The jury was far from impartial. It was made up of well-known, dues-paying artists who taught at a renowned Parisian art school called the École des Beaux Arts (School of Fine Arts). They worked only in artistic styles that society considered acceptable, and they taught their students to follow in their footsteps. If a work did not meet the jury's narrow criteria, it had little to no chance of success.

Criteria for Success

Art historians break these criteria down into several categories. The first concerns a painting's subject matter. In the early 1800s it was considered vulgar to depict common people and themes. Instead, artists were expected to draw inspiration from the great stories of the Bible or Greek and Roman mythology. The most admired artworks showed chubby cherubs, saints at prayer, mighty gods at war or at play, and other classically inspired images—and as far as size went, bigger was always better. These *grandes machines*, as they were called, were the centerpieces of every Salon exhibition.

A second criterion involves the drawing and painting techniques used. At that time every item portrayed in a painting was expected to look as realistic as possible. Only certain paint colors were used, and the illumination was always consistent, as if coming from a bright, unblinking light placed directly in front of the scene. Brushstrokes were expected to be flat and invisible with no ridges showing. Color blending

> **Words in Context**
> *grandes machines*
> Large, elaborate, carefully planned paintings that depict important religious, historic, or mythological scenes.

Japonisme

In 1855 the Japanese port of Yokohama opened to trade with the West. Goods and artifacts from Japan started to flood into all parts of Europe. These items were sold in many Parisian shops. They arrived carefully packed in large crates, nestled among crumpled papers bearing snippets of Japanese artwork.

This packing material turned out to be just as popular as the items it protected. The artists who frequented Japan-themed shops rescued the wadded-up prints and showed them to their friends. These friends, in turn, started to copy the techniques they saw in the delightfully foreign pieces. Before long the Japanese artistic influence was cropping up everywhere—and particularly in the work of the Impressionists.

In an article of the time, writer Theodore Duret explains Japanese artwork's contributions to Impressionism.

> Before Japanese art arrived the painter always lied. Nature, with its bold colors, was there for all to see, but on the canvas all you ever saw were anemic colors. . . . As soon as people looked at Japanese pictures in which the most vivid, piercing colors were set side by side, they finally understood that there were new ways of reproducing certain effects of nature which had been until then considered impossible to reproduce. . . . Japanese art conveys the real appearance of nature by bold new means of coloring, and so strongly influenced the Impressionists.

Along with new color palettes, the Impressionists borrowed other techniques from Japan. They experimented with new perspectives, asymmetrical composition, and new ways of blocking out images. Together, these methods and others lent an Eastern flair to the newest Western art movement.

Quoted in Michael Howard, *Encyclopedia of Impressionism*. London: Carlton, 1997, p. 204.

Pierre-Auguste Renoir, pictured at age thirty-five in this self-portrait, is one of the best-known Impressionist painters. Unlike many of his peers, he chose to display his works in the influential French Salon exhibitions.

and shading were to be perfect. In essence, nothing that indicated the artist's personality, perspective, or even existence was to appear in the finished work.

These restrictive criteria were met with mixed emotions in the artistic community. Some artists fully supported the Salon's approach. They felt that it preserved and protected France's rich artistic traditions. Others, however, felt personally offended by the Salon's narrow focus. They rebelled and refused to conform to the Salon's requirements.

A few artists found a middle ground between these two extremes. Among them was Pierre-Auguste Renoir, who is today one of the most famous Impressionists. Despite his allegiance to the Impressionist group, Renoir also participated in Salon shows throughout his career. His reasons were purely practical. "There are in Paris scarcely fifteen art-lovers capable of liking a painting without Salon approval. There are 80,000 who won't buy so much as a nose from a painter who is not hung at the Salon. That is why I send in two portraits every year,"[3] he explains in a private letter to a friend.

Social Discontent

Renoir was not typical in his dispassionate approach. Most artists either loved the Salon or hated it. As the decades passed the naysayers became more vocal, and criticism of the Salon grew louder and harsher.

This trend was in many ways a sign of the times. Social unrest had been brewing and occasionally erupting in France since the late 1700s, when a decade-long revolution stripped power from the government. This was a welcome change for common French folks, who had had almost no rights under the existing monarchy. After the revolution regular people had a voice for the first time ever—and little by little, they learned to use it. They became more and more willing to speak up about perceived social injustices.

This democratic sensibility was more prevalent after 1848, when another uprising occurred. The people were frustrated by their king, Louis Philippe, who was trying to take back some of the freedoms won in the previous revolution. They responded by tossing the monarch out and sending him to permanent exile in the United Kingdom. They replaced him with an elected president who, they hoped, would recognize the value of the common man.

The Salon, unfortunately, did not seem to recognize this value in the slightest. It celebrated the wealthy and privileged while shunning everyone else. This approach incensed the citizens who were leading the fight for equality. They complained loudly and publicly in newspapers and in flyers. As they did, public sentiment against the Salon grew.

The Salon des Refusés

The situation came to a head in 1863. That year the Salon received about five thousand entries for its exhibition—about double the amount it could accept. When the news emerged that almost twenty-five hundred works had been rejected, a public outcry erupted. People argued that this many artists could not possibly be unworthy. All of the rejected work, they said, should have a chance to be seen, not merely the work deemed acceptable by the Salon.

Napoleon III, then emperor of France, heeded this call, and he issued a surprising declaration. "Numerous complaints have reached the Emperor on the subject of works of art that have been refused by the jury of the exhibition," he writes in a public missive. "His Majesty, wishing to let the public judge the legitimacy of these complaints, has decided that the rejected works of art are to be exhibited in another part of the Palais [Palace]."[4]

The emperor's wishes were carried out. The secondary exhibition, dubbed the Salon des Refusés (Salon of the Refused), was the first official loosening of the Salon's stranglehold on the Parisian art scene. The show was uneven in quality, but it was important nonetheless. It showed exactly how many artists and what styles of art had been censored and suppressed by the Salon. With its massive attendance—much more than the regular Salon show attracted—the exhibition also proved that the public wanted to see new and different types of work.

A New and Different Paris

This attitude echoed larger changes that were being made at this time to the city of Paris itself. Until the early 1850s the city had been a medieval-type settlement with narrow streets, poor sanitation, and no outdoor lighting. As described by one historian, Paris was "dirty, crowded, and unhealthy . . . [c]overed with mud and make-shift shanties, damp and fetid, filled with the signs of poverty as well as the signs of garbage and waste left there by the inadequate and faulty sewer system."[5]

In 1853 Napoleon III decided that this situation was unacceptable. He felt that Paris needed new roads, sewers, lights, housing, and other modern amenities. Declaring that no expense would be spared, Napoleon hired a high-ranking public servant named Baron Georges-Eugène Haussmann to bring his ambitious vision to life.

This decision launched a seventeen-year program of civic improvement known as the Haussmann Plan, which was grander than perhaps anything attempted before or since. Under Baron Haussmann's direction, narrow streets were ripped out and replaced with broad, straight, well-lit boulevards.

Over 27,500 ramshackle houses were knocked down and replaced with modern, multistory apartment blocks. Efficient sewers were installed, tidy embankments were built along river edges, and public parks were created for both beauty and recreation.

These changes and others accomplished Napoleon's goal of modernizing Paris. Their effects, though, reached far beyond the mere cosmetic. When the city's structure changed, its population changed as well. The poverty-stricken people who had occupied Paris's old slums lost their homes and fled to the suburbs. They were replaced by people in better financial circumstances who were eager to live in Haussmann's shiny, clean apartments. New residents flocked to the city in droves, doubling Paris's population from about 1 million to over 2 million between 1851 and 1880. Suddenly the city was packed with people who had plenty of money—and who were eager to spend it.

Businesses of all sorts quickly sprang up to meet this demand. Haussmann's glittering boulevards were soon lined with gourmet restaurants, sidewalk cafés, and fine shops where the bourgeoisie (well-to-do middle-class people) gathered during the day. Later, when the sun went down, cabarets, public houses, fancy theaters, and ballet halls opened their doors to provide a wealth of nightlife options. Offering something for everyone, the newly modernized Paris was a playground that anyone was welcome to enjoy.

Days in the Countryside

The recreation options did not stop in the city's center. Haussmann's changes were designed, in part, to make all parts of Paris easily accessible from all directions. The grand boulevards made it simple to zip to the city's suburbs via horse-drawn carriage or motor vehicle. Also, two new railway stations, the Gare de Lyon and the Gare du Nord, provided public transportation for people who did not have their own conveyances. These changes opened up a world of new opportunities for Parisians of all income levels.

Waterfront fun was one such opportunity. Just outside the city limits, various establishments opened along the River Seine to provide food, public swimming areas, and other options for lazy summer afternoons. A famous example was La Grenouillère, a popular riverside resort on a minor arm of the Seine. Easily accessible by train, the resort was packed with young, fun-loving Parisians whenever the weather was agreeable. This destination was popular among art students and appears in many paintings of the era.

Boating was another popular activity. Whenever they were not working, water lovers fled to surrounding towns like Argenteuil, Pontoise, Bougival, and Chatou to row and sail on pleasant waterways. This type of activity might not seem unusual today, but it was revolutionary at the time. Most Parisians in the previous decades had not had the free time or the money to enjoy themselves in this way. With more affluent inhabitants who could afford more leisure time, there followed a rise in recreational pursuits and hobbies—and the art students of Paris were eager to participate in this new lifestyle. They rowed and sailed along with everyone else. In some instances, these experiences inspired paintings that remain today as records of a long-ago time.

> **Words in Context**
> *bourgeoisie*
> Middle-class people whose lifestyle is based on having ample money and possessions.

Impressionist painters such as Berthe Morisot depicted Parisians engaging in their favorite activities. Morisot's *Reading*, painted in 1873, portrays a solitary woman reading in a forested setting.

Woodland exploration was yet another option for residents of this era. Instead of heading to crowded tourist spots, many people sought the solitude of France's forests. A short train ride brought them to places where they could hike, picnic, or simply relax and enjoy nature. A few decades earlier this option simply had not existed for city dwellers. Now it did, and many people—including painters—eagerly took advantage of this new opportunity.

Another Way of Life

The suburbs and countryside surrounding Paris were undeniably fun, but they offered more than mere entertainment value. For city dwellers they were also windows into another way of life. As the years went by and France's railway system grew, a tourist industry had sprung up to help people explore the country's rural areas. Brochures and guidebooks described quaint villages, inhabitants, and customs in glowing terms. Adventurous Parisians ventured forth to see these places with their own eyes.

Camille Pissarro, Father of Impressionism

In an artistic sense Camille Pissarro is not the most famous of the Impressionists, yet in some ways he was the central member of the group. Often called the Father of Impressionism, Pissarro was the glue that held the group's different and sometimes difficult personalities together.

Pissarro held this position partly because of his age and experience. About ten years older than the other Impressionists, Pissarro had been studying art and experimenting with Impressionist-type techniques for a decade before the rest of the group arrived on the scene. Some younger students were fascinated by Pissarro's work, and they tried their best to emulate it. Additionally, they just liked the older artist. Pissarro was gentle, kind, patient, and friendly. Between his pleasant personality and his innovative art, Pissarro attracted a steady flow of admirers and imitators.

Pissarro turned his following into an artistic movement in 1874, when he spearheaded the first of eight Impressionist exhibitions. He continued these efforts over the next twelve years, mounting seven more shows that featured a variety of Impressionist work. Fiercely committed to the movement's ideals, Pissarro was the only group member who never missed a showing. He did this despite the fact that his work had been shown several times at official Salon shows. But he turned his back on this social acceptance, preferring to follow his personal vision. By doing so, he helped to launch a movement that changed the art world forever.

Art students of the time were just as interested in this aspect of the countryside as anyone. Their goal, though, was a bit different. They wanted not just to see the sights but also to capture them on canvas. On weekends they boarded the train, art supplies in hand, in search of picturesque scenery. When they found what they were looking for, they set up their easels and canvases and went to work.

The images captured in these sessions are interesting to art historians. They tend to be highly idealized—in other words, they show nature as the artist would like it to be and not necessarily as it really was, rife with smoke-spewing factories and smelly sewage plants. This difference is well described by one writer as "the gap between the harassed town-dweller's dream of a clean and innocent natural world as the source of spiritual renewal and the actualities of that landscape."[6] It was an illusion held not only by the artists of the time but also by the general public, who imagined the countryside as a place of perfect peace and beauty. In their approach to rural subjects, painters definitely echoed the sentiments of the era.

Students of Art

This was a new and even shocking development in the eyes of the Parisian art world—and at art schools as well. The official position of the prestigious École des Beaux Arts was that artists were merely technicians preserving an artistic legacy. Their job was to paint specific things in specific ways without letting their personalities or viewpoints show through. When completing assignments, students at the École were not allowed to deviate from this requirement.

This approach had served the École well for a long, long time. But now the times were changing. Ordinary French citizens were starting to think in more independent ways, and many art students felt the same way. In their work they wanted to try new things and explore their own ideas. They did not want to copy old artists, old topics, and old styles. The time had come, they felt, for a revolution not only in France's government but in its artistic styles as well.

This sentiment sparked a major change in Paris's art school scene. Young, talented students knew they would not get any artistic freedom at the École. Instead of applying to the École, therefore, they started to look elsewhere for educational options.

They found it in independent studios called *ateliers*. Ateliers were the workplaces of established, successful artists. These artists often took in students in return for a modest fee or for contributions toward the studio's running costs. They taught their students the basics of life drawing, painting techniques, and other essentials.

Studio "masters" had complete freedom to teach their students in any way they liked, and many were very open to new ideas and experiments. They allowed their pupils a degree of flexibility that they never could have gotten at the École.

Thanks to this approach, the ateliers quickly became popular among less traditionally minded students, including many of the artists who would later emerge as the Impressionists. Claude Monet, Renoir, Frédéric Bazille, and Alfred Sisley, for example, studied together at the atelier of a Swiss artist named Charles Gleyre. Manet worked at a nearby atelier run by painter Thomas Couture. These students and the other future Impressionists worked together, socialized together, and developed their craft together. As the years went by they formed ever tighter personal and professional bonds.

Joining Forces

Common rejection was one of the bonds that these artists shared. Most of the future Impressionists submitted work to the Salon's jury each year in hope of being accepted into the big show. With a very few exceptions, these attempts failed. Despite their many merits, Impressionist-style works were repeatedly rejected by the Salon.

As the years went by and this rejection continued, young artists felt more and more frustrated. They were angry with the art establishment's conservative attitudes. They were also convinced of their own talent, skill, and vision. All they needed, they thought, was a chance—just one chance—to show the world what they could do.

At this point it seemed obvious to most of the future Impressionists that their chance would not come from the Salon. They would have to find a different way to show their work to the public. To accomplish this goal they decided to form a business partnership, which they dubbed the Société Anonyme des Peintres, Sculpteurs, Graveurs, etc. (Anonymous Society of Painters, Sculptors, Engravers, etc.). The group would organize and run its own exhibitions completely independent of the Salon and its old-fashioned standards.

A nineteenth-century art studio (pictured) provides a place for students to explore new styles and techniques. Many of the Impressionists who would one day become famous developed their craft in independent studios such as this.

In a letter to his family, Bazille sums up the situation. He describes his own feelings along with those of his friends Monet, Renoir, and Sisley as he writes:

I shan't send anything more to the jury. It is far too ridiculous. . . . What I say here, a dozen young people of talent think along with me. We have therefore decided to rent each year a large studio where we'll exhibit as many of our works as we wish. We shall invite painters whom we like to send us pictures. [Jean Désiré Gustave] Courbet, [Jean-Baptiste-Camille] Corot, [Narcisse Virgilio] Diaz, [Charles-François] Daubigny, and many others . . . have promised to send pictures and very much approve of our idea. With these people, and Monet, who is stronger than all of them, we are sure to succeed. You shall see that we'll be talked about.[7]

Independent Exhibitions

Bazille was right in some ways. The Société's first show was certainly talked about after it opened on April 15, 1874. Most of the talk, however, was negative. Critics and the public had harsh words for the works of art on display. The exhibiting artists, including Renoir, Monet, Camille Pissarro, Edgar Degas, Sisley, and Berthe Morisot, were personally criticized as well. In the end, the show was a critical and commercial flop.

The artists of the Société, however, refused to be discouraged. They vowed to continue their efforts in the years to come. Between 1874 and 1886 the group mounted seven more exhibitions. These events did not focus on Impressionist-style work; they featured many different artists working with many approaches. The Impressionist theme, however, was a constant thread. Over time the public and critics alike grew accustomed—or perhaps resigned—to this artistic style.

Increasing acceptance, however, could not hold the Société together. By the time of the group's last exhibition, many original core members had started experimenting with new styles and markets.

They had little interest in the Société's shows, and they did not participate. In addition, tensions had arisen over the years between even the Société's most devoted members. Tired and depleted, the group dissolved its official bonds after the 1886 exhibition.

The group's impact, however, lived on. In twelve short years, the Impressionists had done exactly what they had set out to do: They had managed to change the way the world thought about art. These efforts benefited the group's individual members later, as they took their careers in different directions. Some of the artists found popular success, while others did not. All, however, are now recognized for the important roles they played in art history. Together, this group of people looked at their changing world in a new way—and they made others do the same. In the process, they launched the most revolutionary movement the art world has ever seen.

Chapter Two

Tools and Techniques

In 1858 a young Claude Monet was just starting his artistic training. Monet's mentor at the time, Eugène Boudin, encouraged the seventeen-year-old student to abandon the studio and instead paint outdoors. Monet followed Boudin's advice—and this activity, Monet recalled years later, completely changed his artistic approach. "All of a sudden it was like a veil torn from my eyes and I understood at last. I realized what painting could be. My own destiny as a painter opened up before me,"[8] he said.

In this quotation Monet is referring to the difference between seeing something—really *seeing* it, with one's own eyes—and simply remembering it. The distinction is important because artists of the time usually worked in studios, drawing their inspiration from sketches or mere memory. Their work, not surprisingly, often lacked vitality as a result. Paintings done *en plein air*, or out of doors, on the other hand, had a better chance of capturing true-to-life colors, shadows, and shapes. Because images passed straight from the artist's eye to the hand and then onto the canvas, this simple technique could yield astonishing results.

Monet was not the only Impressionist to discover the benefits of working en plein air. This habit was adopted by all within Monet's circle to greater or lesser degrees. It is responsible in large part for the realism that is a hallmark of Impressionist-style work, and it is remembered today as perhaps the Impressionists' signature technique.

It is not, however, Impressionism's only innovation. The Impressionists were experimenters at heart, and they tried all sorts of new things in their work. They combined newly available art tools with frowned-upon or untried methods to produce works of startling originality. Studying the Impressionists' tools and techniques is helpful in understanding the finished products that seem so familiar today but were so revolutionary in their own era.

Outdoor Tools

Artists prior to the Impressionist era did not work indoors solely because they wanted to. They did it in large part because their supplies were cumbersome and difficult to transport. One such item was the easel, a wooden device made to hold works in progress. Traditional easels were large, heavy, and sturdy, designed to hold the huge canvases so popular at the time. Carrying these easels outdoors was difficult or even impossible, so artists stayed inside.

> **Words in Context**
> *en plein air*
> French for *in open air*, the Impressionists' favorite way of working.

Paints were another troublesome item. Through the early 1800s paint was available only as a dry powder called pigment. The artist mixed various pigments with oil and with each other to create the shades he or she needed. The process was delicate, time-consuming, and hard to get exactly right. Also, because paints were mixed directly on boards called palettes, they could not be stored. They dried out quickly, especially outdoors. This made them impractical for out-of-studio work.

Starting around 1840, though, many new options became available on the art supply market. Premixed paints in metal tubes were perhaps the most helpful of these options. Manufactured in large batches, these paints were always a predictable color, unlike the hand-mixed variety. Even better, their resealable tubes made it simple to squeeze out a quick dab of paint whenever it was needed. With no mixing hassles, drying-out issues, or mess, tubes of paint were an outdoor artist's dream.

Portable easels helped, too. With the rising popularity of landscape painting, suppliers saw the need for smaller, foldable easels that were easy to carry from one place to another. They quickly developed and sold these handy devices. Portable easels were an instant hit with the Impressionists, who liked to settle down and start painting wherever and whenever inspiration struck.

This convenience came at a cost. Historians agree that in taking advantage of modern tools, the Impressionists failed to learn some skills that were considered essential at the time, particularly the proper mixing of colors. As one writer points out, "Even artists who had received a thorough training, like [Pierre-Auguste] Renoir and [Edgar] Degas, felt a deep unease with their level of technical expertise."[9] This unease, though, did not stop the Impressionists from pursuing their craft. They forged ahead with an enthusiasm that, they hoped, would make up for any technical deficiencies.

Premixed paints in metal tubes gave artists more flexibility to work outdoors. Earlier artists had to spend hours mixing powdered pigments that dried out quickly and, once combined, did not always result in the desired colors.

Slapping It On

This enthusiasm came across, in part, in the methods the Impressionists used to apply their paints. Before the Impressionist era emphasis had been placed on careful brushwork that left no texture or stroke marks. The Impressionists, however, largely abandoned this approach. They slapped paint onto canvas with palette knives, coarse brushes, and any other implements that struck their fancy. Working quickly and exuberantly, they left all sorts of brushstrokes and textures visible in their works.

The two effects—strokes and texture—are related, but not the same. Flat but individually visible brushstrokes are known as broken color or broken brushstrokes. Painted skillfully, many broken brushstrokes can work together to depict an image. It is easy to see exactly how the painter constructed the image; the types of tools used, precise paint shades, and other technical details are clearly evident in the finished product.

Textured areas of a painting also reveal brushstrokes, but they have other visual effects as well. They add character to certain objects and details. They also reflect light off the painting's surface in interesting ways. The application of thick, raised paint, which is known as impasto, was used to good effect by most Impressionist artists.

An example of this approach can be seen in Renoir's painting *Two Sisters* (1881). In this painting a teenage girl and her younger sister sit on a terrace overlooking a lake. The older sister has apparently been doing some knitting, because a basket full of yarn balls sits on her lap. In contrast to the sisters' faces and hands, which are painted with smooth, invisible brushstrokes, the yarn balls are bold and textured. They seem to have some of the texture of real yarn. This detail is small, but it is effective. It adds a touch of realism that helps bring Renoir's painting to life.

This realism was not always appreciated by critics of the era. Many found it sloppy and unfinished. Other viewers, however, thought the new techniques had interesting possibilities. Critic

Ernest Chesneau offers the following words about *Boulevard des Capucines* (1873), a work by Monet: "From a distance, this stream of life, this great shimmering of light and shade, spangled with brighter light and stronger shade, must be saluted as a masterpiece. As you approach, everything vanishes; all that remains is an indecipherable chaos of palette scrapings."[10] For this critic, at least, the casual brushwork now seen as a characteristic of Impressionist painting made a mesmerizing impact.

Technique That Tells a Story

This type of impact was not accidental. The Impressionists' brushstrokes may have seemed haphazard to some observers, but in actuality they were carefully chosen to produce certain effects.

The impression of motion was one such effect. Hurried, slanted strokes, for instance, might convey the idea of reeds bending in a strong wind. More delicate, rounded strokes might mimic gently spreading ripples on a pond's surface. Artists used each stroke's width, length, and shape to enhance the story they were trying to tell.

Along with motion, brushstrokes were also used to convey mood. A tranquil scene, for example, might be depicted with calm, measured strokes. A busy or emotionally charged scene, on the other hand, might be better communicated through a hastier approach. A good example is Monet's painting *La Rue Saint-Denis, fête du 30 juin 1878* (1878). This painting is an overhead view of a street bedecked with waving flags. With a blocky, hurried appearance, the scene crackles with energy. "The pulsating color of the dazzling flags is matched by an almost frenzied brushstroke, conveying an excitement equivalent to the mood of the holiday that inspired it,"[11] comments one writer.

> **Words in Context**
> *impasto*
> A painting technique that involves the application of thick, raised paint.

Assigning importance to various parts of a painting was yet another task the Impressionists managed through brushwork. Objects that the artist wanted to emphasize were carefully painted and given plenty of detail. Objects that the artist felt were unimportant, on the other hand, were practically ignored. They were merely sketched in with a few rough swipes of the brush. By varying their brushwork in this way, artists made their central themes obvious to every viewer.

As was true of most aspects of Impressionist work, this technique was criticized when it first came into use. The prevailing attitude comes through in a comment written about the Impressionist artist Berthe Morisot. "That young lady is not interested in reproducing trifling details," sneered the author. "When she has a hand to paint, she makes exactly as many brushstrokes lengthwise as there are fingers, and the business is done."[12]

This critic was missing the point. Morisot, like most of the Impressionists, *was* interested in reproducing details—but only the ones she cared about. If a subject's hand was not important to her message, she saw no need to devote much time or attention to it. Let the viewer focus elsewhere, on the images Morisot rendered faithfully and which she considered central to her theme.

A close-up view of Monet's *Water Lilies* reveals coarse brush strokes and texture, neither of which would have been acceptable in paintings of the past. Impressionist artists used these techniques to convey motion and mood.

A White Canvas

Rendering an impression required more than just paint texture and fancy brushwork. It also took a keen eye for color—and because the Impressionists were working in such innovative ways, traditional color theories and methods did not always suit their needs. They had to come up with fresh approaches to this artistic task.

One fundamental issue the Impressionists faced was the need for light, bright tones in their work. They were trying to capture the true colors of nature, not the subdued shades so common for studio painters of the time. To depict indoor lighting and bring depth to their paintings, traditionally minded artists prepared their canvases by precoating them with brown or other somber shades. These dark backgrounds were undeniably rich, but they tended to dampen bright colors.

To solve this problem, the Impressionists started with light-colored canvases instead of dark ones. They achieved this by washing each work surface with white or cream-colored pigment before settling down to work. This background brightened the overall look of finished work in a couple of ways. If a certain paint or color was even a little bit translucent, the white canvas showed through, brightening the overall tone in that area. For an even sharper splash of white, the artist could simply skip painting a certain spot. By allowing the pure tone of the canvas to appear, the painter could achieve a brilliance that was not possible on a brown background.

This technique, like so many the Impressionists pioneered, was considered unusual in the mid-1800s. Over time, though, it caused a permanent shift in the art world. Today every art supply store stocks piles of prepared white canvases. If artists want a canvas of any other color they must do the base coat themselves. Thanks to the Impressionists, white is now the standard starting point for painters working in any artistic style.

Complementary Colors

Using white canvases was just the beginning of the Impressionists' innovations. These artists found that they could not re-create

Lois Griffel, Modern Impressionist

Since her early childhood in the 1950s American artist Lois Griffel has been fascinated with light and color. This fascination eventually led Griffel to art school, to various jobs as a working artist, and later to the Cape Cod School of Art in Provincetown, Massachusetts. There, Griffel not only learned but mastered the techniques of Impressionism. Today Griffel holds the title of Master Signature Member from the American Impressionist Society.

In a magazine profile Griffel shares her thoughts about working in the Impressionist style. "In order to see and paint atmosphere, one must understand that when we first view something, we see large patterns of lights and darks before we notice details," she says. "For example, when we recognize a friend walking toward us, we first recognize the shape of his or her body and face before we notice his or her shoes or jewelry. As the person comes closer, some details gradually become more obvious, and we may take note of the hair and eye color. Finally we may observe how the warm orange color of his or her shirt clashes with the cool aqua hue of his or her pants."

According to Griffel, this way of seeing things is much more than just an artistic trick. It is a talent—and a great gift as well. "The greatest gift we are given as artists is the ability to see the infinite variety of color in nature. Impressionism is not a way to paint but a way to see . . . [it is] a method for translating what we see into paint," she says.

Lois Griffel, "A Modern Approach to Studying Light and Color," *Painting the Impressionist Landscape, Articles and Essays.* www.loisgriffel.com.

the light effects and colors of nature using traditional academic color techniques. They had to come up with new methods, and they turned to a chemist named Michel-Eugène Chevreul for inspiration.

Chevreul had earned recognition in 1839 with the publication of a book entitled *On the Law of Simultaneous Contrast of Colors*. The idea that formed the basis of this book was born when Chevreul, who worked with dyes at a textile factory, noticed that fabrics seemed to take on different colors depending on their surroundings. After years of observation, experimentation, and color demonstrations, Chevreul came up with a law that he dubbed the *simultaneous contrast of colors*. "In the case where the eye sees at the same time two contiguous colors, they will appear as dissimilar as possible, both in their optical composition [hue] and in the height of their tone [mixture with white or black],"[13] the law states.

In simpler terms, Chevreul is saying that side-by-side colors have a boosting effect on each other. He found that the effect was greatest between complementary colors: blue and orange, red and green, yellow and purple. The contrast produced by these pairs, says Chevreul, is "superior to every other."[14] In his book the scientist presents charts, images, and copious notes to support his findings.

The Impressionists were not the first artists to discover Chevreul's writings or to admire them. They were among the earliest, though, to enthusiastically adopt these color theories in their work. An example appears in Camille Pissarro's *Peasant Women Planting Pea Sticks* (1890). In this rural farm scene, a group of women works in a lush green field. The central figure wears a bright red scarf and skirt that stand out vividly against the green background. The contrast pulls the viewer's eye directly to the center of the painting and the heart of the action, exactly as the artist no doubt intended.

Optical Blending

Chevreul's findings were not restricted to contrasting colors. They concerned the harmonious blending of shades as well. During his research, Chevreul discovered that blocks of color, when placed next to each other, seemed to mingle and form a third color. Blues and yellows together, for instance, produced the impression of green, while reds and yellows created an orange overtone. This effect is called optical blending or optical mixing, and it is a cornerstone of Impressionist art.

Before learning how the Impressionists used this technique, it is important to understand how it works. Optical blending is a function of the human eyes and brain, not the colors themselves. It occurs whenever a person sees side-by-side color blocks. Instead of seeing the individual colors, the viewer perceives one color that is a mixture of the others. The effect is greatest at a distance, when color blocks appear smaller and harder to pick apart. A modern-day example of this principle is seen in television images, which mix tiny dots of red, blue, and green light to produce every color viewers see on the TV screen.

Optical blending was not well understood or much practiced prior to the Impressionist era. Instead of using this technique, traditional artists painstakingly mixed pigments to create solid shades. They might achieve an exact lavender, for instance, with a careful blend of red, blue, and white. Or they might spend hours mixing blues and yellows to make a variety of greens. A skilled colorist could produce just about any shade using this method. But the process was time-consuming, and the pigments lost much of their intensity when combined.

The Impressionists took a different approach. Instead of blending pigments, they applied vibrant streaks, dashes, and dots of pure color to their canvases. They carefully arranged these colors to produce the visual effects they wanted. By working in this way, the Impressionists kept their colors undiluted and created a brighter overall effect in their work.

In his journal the French artist Eugène Delacroix comments on the optical blending he observed in a much lauded painting

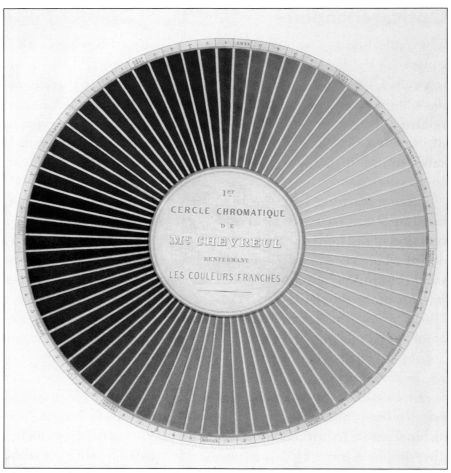

The French chemist Michel-Eugène Chevreul used this color wheel and other images to explain the effect of placing one color next to another. He found that side-by-side colors have a boosting effect on each other.

entitled *The Hay Wain* (1824) by John Constable. "[Constable] says that the superiority of green in his meadows stems from the fact that it consists of a host of different greens," Delacroix says. "The error of intensity and of life in the greenness painted by the average landscape artist is the result of his usually employing a uniform tone. What he says here about the green of the meadows can be applied to every tone."[15]

Banning Black

The Impressionists took this concept to heart and applied it to all of their work. In doing so they became keenly aware of the true colors of the outdoor world instead of the idealized tones and shades produced indoors. As their skills grew, the artists noticed something interesting: Black was seldom seen in nature. Even the darkest object, observed carefully, was built of blocks, lines, and dashes of myriad subdued colors.

The Impressionists embraced this finding. They started experimenting enthusiastically with ways to create dark effects using bright colors. Most of them, in fact, banned black paint from their palettes altogether. Renoir, for example, restricted his palette to seven basic colors: lead white, a bright red called vermilion, a rich rose shade, emerald green, two types of blue, and a brilliant yellow. He was able to produce every effect he wanted using these simple pigments.

One of the Impressionists' key observations concerned the general tones of shadows. They realized, through repeated observation, that an object's shadow contained mostly the object's complementary shade. This meant that red objects, for instance, cast greenish shadows. Yellow objects cast purplish shadows, and blue objects cast orangey shadows. By using dabs of the appropriate complementary color, artists could paint shadows that were more realistic than any black blob could ever be.

> **Words in Context**
> *complementary*
> Colors that produce a neutral color when mixed in certain proportions. Side-by-side blocks of complementary colors contrast strongly.

The Impressionists' shadows were not only more realistic than the traditional black variety. They had much more visual impact, too. A modern art theorist explains why. "The Impressionists avoided black not only because it nearly doesn't exist in nature, but because the effects caused by changes in hue [undiluted color] are so much richer than those caused by changes in shade [colors mixed with black]," he says. "When you use pure black to create contrast, you miss out completely on the powerful effects of changes in hue."[16]

Paintings as Snapshots

The art of photography was developed in France in the mid-1800s. The technology was an instant smash hit with the public, who loved this new way of capturing scenes from everyday life.

Many visual artists, including the Impressionists, also loved the new medium. They realized that photography offered fresh ways to see the world, and they took full advantage of this fact. Edgar Degas, Claude Monet, Charles Gleyre, Édouard Manet, and other artists of the time used cameras to capture scenes that they studied and painted later.

This method led to many of the techniques that characterize Impressionist painting. Like the snapshots of the day, the Impressionists' images often feature cut-off or blurry figures. They are full of life and movement, as though they are moments frozen in time. They may also be packed with insignificant details in a way that previous art was not. Viewing a photograph, a modern artist could take the time to notice things that a studio painter might not think to include in a carefully planned-out scene.

The use of photography led, too, to increased accuracy in the poses of people and creatures. Degas, for example, studied photographs of galloping horses to understand the exact position of the animals' legs, hooves, neck, and tail. He used this knowledge to paint stunningly realistic racetrack scenes. Without photography, this type of precision would not have been possible.

The Impressionists may not have understood all of the scientific reasons for this effect, but that did not matter. They saw that it existed, and they took full advantage of it in their work. Today, the absence of pure black is recognized as a hallmark of Impressionist painting.

Capture the Moment

The Impressionists did not experiment with colors just for fun. They did it because they were striving to capture fleeting moments in time. For the same reason, the Impressionists also developed speedier ways of working. This change affected the Impressionists' artistic products in ways that were very recognizable at the time and are still very recognizable today.

The best known effect was the Impressionists' tendency to simplify images. Whereas the old masters might have spent days perfecting a tiny detail, the Impressionists were content to merely hint at many things. The overall feeling of the work—the *impression*—was much more important to these artists than technical precision. The end result was a look that some critics felt was haphazard and hurried, but which had a raw immediacy lacking in more painstaking works.

The Impressionists' tendency to simplify also applied to composition. Traditional artists often spent weeks making sketches and planning out each piece before setting brush to canvas. They carefully arranged the elements of their work to produce a certain effect. The Impressionists, in contrast, were painting real scenes—things they actually observed with their own eyes. The composition therefore was whatever it was, and the artist had no say in the matter. This way of working led to much simpler and much more realistic presentations.

It also led to smaller canvases. Traditional artists had favored huge works, considering them more impressive and important than modest paintings. Unlike sketches, though, reality did not freeze and

> **Words in Context**
> *optical blending* or *mixing*
> A color mixing effect created not by actually mixing pigments but by placing colors side by side in such a way that the viewer's eye creates the desired blend.

allow the artist to take his or her time. It changed quickly—and the Impressionist style, accordingly, had to be quick as well. Using smaller formats made it much easier for the artist to capture the desired scene.

Together, smaller canvases and speedier methods had an interesting side effect: They allowed the Impressionists to finish vast amounts of work. Monet, for example, produced about twenty-five hundred paintings, drawings, and pastels, and Renoir is credited with over six thousand works. The other Impressionists, while not quite as prolific, also left healthy collections. This abundance undoubtedly helped the Impressionist movement to reach its current popularity. Today, museums display many thousands of Impressionist paintings for art lovers to study and enjoy.

Chapter Three

Capturing the Light

The French Impressionists were passionate about many aspects of their work. When it came to capturing light effects, though, this passion was so intense that it sometimes bordered on obsession. The Impressionists painted the way sunlight reflected off water and the way shadows dappled people's bodies. They observed the lighting changes that occurred when a cloud passed overhead, or when the seasons shifted, or when candles flickered at night. These circumstances and many, many others enthralled the Impressionists and gave them never-ending chances to practice their observation and painting skills.

This dogged practice, historians agree, had the desired effect. In their own ways, all of the Impressionists became very good at portraying light effects. Their methods were unfamiliar to the art establishment and to viewers and, like most things the Impressionists did, were met with a great deal of criticism. However, some applauded their work. "[The Impressionists] have . . . succeeded in breaking down sunlight into its rays, its elements, and to reconstitute its unity by means of the general harmony of spectrum colors which they spread on their canvases," raves art critic Edmond Duranty. "The most learned physicist could find nothing to criticize in their analysis of light."[17]

Modern audiences would tend to agree. Art lovers around the world marvel to this day at the Impressionists' ability to bring light to life. Whether painting indoors or outdoors, day or night, summer or winter, these artists understood and captured the ever-changing nuances of light and shadow.

The Colors of Light and Shadow

One simple discovery was the basis of the Impressionists' success. In their quest to paint reality, these artists quickly realized that light and shadows did not consist of solid colors. In other words, a green tree was not just green, and a red hat was not just red. Observed carefully, these objects and all others were seen to be blends of countless shades. By opening their eyes and their minds to the world's true appearance, the Impressionists were able to capture these real and sometimes startling color combinations.

One of Pierre-Auguste Renoir's most famous paintings, *Dance at Le Moulin de la Galette* (1876), offers a remarkable example of this approach. In this work, a crowd of happy people gather at an outdoor dance venue on a sunny afternoon. Beneath the trees the revelers dance, eat, drink, and chat. The sunlight peeks through the tree branches that shade the dance floor, creating splotches of random bright light in some places and throwing other areas into deep shade. The effect should be busy and confusing—but it is not. The result is instantly recognizable as dappled sunlight, and the colors seem so real that viewers are instantly drawn into the painting.

As was true of most Impressionist techniques, this type of realism was not always appreciated. An art critic named Albert Wolff huffed after seeing one of Renoir's paintings, "Try to explain to M. Renoir that a woman's torso is not a mass of flesh in the process of decomposition with green and violet spots."[18]

Wolff was right in his own way, of course. Human flesh is not actually green and violet. But Renoir and the other Impressionists sought a deeper truth. By depicting light's play on objects, they captured what people actually saw instead of what they thought they saw, which was not always the same thing. Part reality and part optical illusion, Impressionist works brought light's colors to life in a totally new way.

Light on the Landscape

This technique was very effective in landscape painting. Plunking themselves and their canvases in the midst of the natural world, the Impressionists struggled to capture the ever-changing play of light on the land.

Camille Pissarro was the first Impressionist to become seriously interested in this pursuit. He liked the work of earlier landscape artists, who made outdoor sketches and then finished their work indoors—but he thought he could do better. He wanted to capture the shifting light exactly as he saw it with his own eyes. Instead of working in a studio, therefore, Pissarro stayed outdoors until he completed each piece. By doing so, he was able to reproduce light effects with a realism never before seen. He earned a reputation as a great landscapist as a result.

The Impressionists understood that they could recreate light and shadows by blending many shades of color. This is how Renoir created a feeling of dappled sunlight in his *Dance at Le Moulin de la Galette* (pictured).

Alfred Sisley, too, relished the challenges of landscape painting. He spent most of his time painting outdoor scenes. Over time he became proficient at painting the shifting sunlight and shadows of the outdoor world.

Sisley's painting *The Effect of Snow at Argenteuil* (1874) demonstrates the artist's mastery of outdoor light. In this work, golden sunlight illuminates a pocked, pitted snowbank next to a road. The bright snow contrasts starkly with the shadow cast by the raised roadway. The colors of the ground, sky, and distant forests are perfect, giving the viewer the unshakeable impression of a chilly but pleasant day. The elongated shadows and the sunset-tinged clouds clearly communicate a late afternoon feeling that is instantly and unmistakably recognizable.

It is interesting to note Sisley's use of complementary colors in this work. The sunlit snow has an orange hue, while the shadowed snow appears blue. These adjacent fields of color contrast starkly, giving the area a strong visual pull. The viewer's eye goes straight to the snowy ground, exactly as Sisley intended.

Sunlight on Water

While Sisley worked on his landscapes, other Impressionists took up an even more difficult task. They became determined to capture the exact ways that sunlight and reflections bounced off water. Most water is in constant motion, alive with ripples and waves that reflect the light differently from one second to the next. The Impressionists recognized the impossibility of painting these images with precise accuracy. Their goal, instead, was to capture the overall visual impression the water created.

They did this in large part through their use of color. Depending on the lighting conditions and the nearby objects, a body of water might reflect any number of hues. Each individual flash of color came and went quickly, but the same colors tended to appear over and over again in different places. A skillful artist could use the broken color technique to mimic the overall colors and the balance of the individual flashes. Viewed together, the different colors combined to capture the look and feeling of real water.

Many Impressionists incorporated water into their work. The undisputed master of the genre, though, was Claude Monet. Monet was fascinated by water throughout his working life. He painted it over and over in different weather and light conditions. He returned to certain places many times, capturing the same scenes at different angles and with different color schemes, depending on what he observed.

One of Monet's frequent subjects was the bridge at Argenteuil, just outside of Paris. Monet had a favorite riverbank where he sat and

Alfred Sisley's *The Effect of Snow at Argenteuil* (pictured) reveals the artist's mastery of outdoor light. The colors used to create sunlit snow, sunset-tinged clouds, and distant forests clearly leave the impression of a chilly but pleasant day.

Floating Studios

Some artists were experimenting with light effects before the Impressionist movement began. A notable example is Charles-François Daubigny (1817–1878). Daubigny was so interested in the play of sunlight on water that in 1857 he built a floating studio so he could study the effect more closely. Dubbed *Le Botin*, Daubigny's unusual work space gave him a new perspective on watery subjects.

Daubigny did not merely paint on *Le Botin*. He also entertained other artists, including a young Claude Monet. Daubigny was eager to share his approach with the young Impressionists and to learn from them as well.

Monet's outings with Daubigny made a lasting impression. Nearly two decades later, in 1874, Monet followed the older artist's example and created his own floating studio. He used this vessel to find and capture visual angles he could not have achieved from shore. In addition, Monet observed that the quality of the light on the water looked different from the floating studio. Reflected from a mere arm's length away, the water's shimmers and sparkles had a completely different size, shape, and brightness than they did from shore.

Art historians agree that the Impressionists' boat-based work has some qualities not seen in other works. The canvases tend to be smaller, the brushstrokes are more rushed, and the colors are brighter. Whether these differences arose from the working conditions, the changed perspective, or both, they mark a unique entry in the Impressionist catalog.

painted the bridge along with nearby boats, buildings, and trees. The River Seine, which flowed beneath the bridge, is the focus of these works. The water sparkles with bright bursts of light in some paintings. In others, it reflects mellower shades. Regardless of the lighting conditions, all of the Argenteuil works capture the essence of the river at a single moment in time.

Émile Zola, a famous novelist and art critic, publicly lauded Monet's remarkable ability to paint water. "With him, water is alive, deep, above all it is real. It laps against the boats with little greenish ripples cut across with white flashes: it spreads out in glaucous [bluish-gray] pools, suddenly ruffled by a breeze, it lengthens the masts reflected on its surface by breaking up their image, it has dull and lambent tints lit up by broken gleams of light,"[19] he writes. This comment shows that Zola, like many other viewers, was impressed with this aspect of the Impressionists' work.

> **Words in Context**
> *reflect*
> To cast light back from a surface; depending on the surface, this light can be a pure color, a collection of broken colors, or a coherent image.

Light over Time

Monet's multiple paintings of the Argenteuil Bridge were not simply studies of light on water. They were also studies of the way light conditions change over time. The Impressionists understood that morning light was different from afternoon or evening light, and that bright light was different from dim light. They saw that the quality of the light at any given moment completely changed the appearance of the objects it illuminated, and they were eager to capture these changes on canvas.

Monet was more consumed with this challenge than any of the other Impressionists. He had a well-known habit of painting the same subjects over and over to capture lighting nuances between different moments. Because conditions could change so quickly—say, when a cloud drifted across the sky and covered the sun—Monet often worked on several canvases at the same time. While bright sunlight prevailed, Monet worked feverishly on a painting with a sunny theme. When the sky clouded over, he snatched up a cloudy canvas and worked on that one instead. He might make this switch dozens of times in the course of an afternoon's work.

This obsession reached its peak in Monet's *Rouen Cathedral* series, which was completed between 1892 and 1893. The more than thirty paintings that the series comprises depict the historic cathedral in the town of Rouen, France. All of the works feature the same view of the building under different lighting conditions. The view is the same because to get close to the building, Monet rented a second-floor room across the street. He set up several easels by the room's windows and moved from canvas to canvas throughout the day as the light changed.

The *Rouen* series reveals many interesting things about sunlight's changing qualities. Art critics comment in particular about the effect produced by full, bright sunlight falling on objects. Duranty summarized this effect when he wrote of the Impressionists' work, "Their discovery actually consists in having recognized that full light de-colors tones, that the sun reflected by objects tends (because of its brightness) to bring them back to that luminous unity which melts its seven prismatic rays into a single colorless radiance: light."[20] In the Rouen series and other works, the Impressionists used this brilliant whiteness to striking effect.

Changing Seasons

In their quest to capture light effects, the Impressionists did not focus solely on hour-to-hour changes. They took a broader view as well. They noticed that lighting conditions shifted not only with the time of day but also with the seasons—and as with all things light-related, the Impressionists were determined to capture these shifts on canvas.

All of the Impressionists experimented with seasonal lighting. But once again it is Monet, the master of light effects, who

The Unwilling Impressionist

Edgar Degas is included on virtually every list of Impressionist painters. He earns this spot for many reasons. His subject matter, his use of color, and his photographic-type composition identify him with the Impressionist camp. Degas was also part of the Impressionist social group, and he exhibited work in seven of the eight Impressionist exhibitions.

Despite these ties, though, Degas never considered himself an Impressionist. In fact, it made him angry when people tried to associate him with the group. He called himself a Realist instead—a term that, to him, implied a careful and highly technical approach to painting. "No art was ever less spontaneous than mine. What I do is the result of reflection and study of the great masters; of inspiration, spontaneity, temperament . . . I know nothing," Degas once famously said.

One aspect of this approach was Degas's refusal to work en plein air as did his enthusiastically Impressionist colleagues. When planning most of his famous dancing scenes, Degas brought models to his studio. He sketched them over and over in different poses. Then he patiently worked these sketches into compositions that captured a feeling of spontaneity but which, in reality, were anything but spontaneous. In this sense, Degas was indeed distant from his Impressionist peers.

Still, Degas made an important contribution to the Impressionist oeuvre. His study of theatrical lighting and his experiments in capturing it were influential both in his own time and in years to come.

Quoted in Carol M. Armstrong, *Odd Man Out: Readings of the Work and Reputation of Edgar Degas.* Los Angeles, CA: Getty Publications, 2003, p. 22.

produced the defining example of this approach. Monet's *Haystacks* series was painted from the late summer of 1890 through the spring of 1891, thus spanning all four seasons. The paintings in the series focus on large haystacks that stood in fields near Monet's Giverny home. Monet's correspondence from this period shows that he set out to paint only a few haystacks, but ended up becoming obsessed with the project. "The further I get, the more I see how much work it will need to convey what I am searching for,"[21] he moans in a letter to a friend.

Monet's obsession resulted in twenty-five paintings that portray haystacks in the morning, afternoon, and evening at different times of the year. Some haystacks reflect the rich light of an autumn afternoon. Others stand stark against fields bursting with spring flowers. Still others sag beneath the weight of snowdrifts, weakly illuminated by winter's dim sunshine. The winter paintings seem to have been especially difficult due to daylight's short duration. "At this season the sun is sinking so quickly that I can't follow it,"[22] Monet complains.

Monet may not have been fully satisfied with his work. Viewers, however, hailed the series as masterful when it was exhibited in May of 1891. Critics raved about the paintings: their colors, their scope, their overall feeling, and much more. The exhibition was not only a critical smash but a commercial success as well, completely selling out within a few days. In this regard, the series was a turning point both for Monet professionally and for Impressionism in general.

Sunlight on People

While Sisley, Monet, and Pissarro strove to paint nature in its simple glory, other Impressionists had different goals. They were much more interested in the way sunlight played and danced upon people and their activities.

Of all the Impressionists, Renoir is best known for this type of focus. Renoir was a friendly, energetic, sociable man who loved Paris and its crowded streets, parks, and cafés. He lived in a small room overlooking the Pont Neuf, a bridge across the River Seine in the heart of the city. From his window Renoir could paint the hustle and bustle of the pedestrians and traffic passing below. When he got bored, he could visit local entertainment spots to paint in the thick of the action.

As was true of Impressionist work in general, Renoir's subject matter was not usually the main point of a painting. More important by far was the lighting of whatever Renoir chose to portray. A view of the Pont Neuf, for example, might showcase the way people and their shadows appeared in the harsh midday sun. A scene of happy revelers on the Seine might show some people in light and others in shadow as their boat passed below a shady tree.

Renoir's effort to capture the interplay of light and shadow is especially obvious in a famous work entitled *La Balançoire* (1876). The central image in this painting is a young woman in a long white dress standing on a wooden swing. Two men and a child stand near the swinging woman; other people linger in the far background. None of the people seem to be doing anything in particular. They are all simply enjoying a lazy moment along a sun-stippled forest path. One art historian aptly describes the subject of the painting as "the human figure seen in light and in half-shadow, under trees. In this later work, the men, the woman, and the little girl, without entirely losing their substantiality, entirely lack . . . presence. They are clearly subordinated to the overall play of dappled light."[23]

> **Words in Context**
> *dappled*
> Having spots of a different shade, tone, or color from the background; mottled.

This painting and others by Renoir are often mentioned as the best examples of rendering sunlight on people. They are not, however, the only ones. Other Impressionists tackled this challenge as well. Berthe Morisot, for instance, painted many interesting studies of sunlight falling on the human body, and Édouard Manet loved to paint horse races and other outdoor activity. In all of these works, the light is a character just as real—and sometimes more so—than the living beings portrayed.

Indoor Lighting

Although the Impressionists were primarily fascinated by outdoor sunlight, they did not neglect other types of lighting. Many Impressionist works feature indoor scenes. These paintings were carefully executed to showcase not only certain places, objects, and people but also the lighting effects of the surroundings.

One such effect was indoor sunlight—in other words, rooms illuminated through windows or doors by the sun shining outside. The feeling and overall tone of these scenes varied greatly depending on the circumstances. Sunbeams shining directly into a room, for instance, affected the look of things in a very different way than indirect sunlight did. The time of day, the weather outside, and the season all played important parts as well. Inside as well as outside, the Impressionists could explore infinite nuances of light and shade.

This type of work was practical during daytime hours. But the sun inevitably set each day—and when it did, many of the Impressionists abandoned the pursuit of sunlight and turned to artificially lit scenes instead. The theater, with its lush chandeliers, candles, and other illuminations, was a favorite subject. Patrons are shown sometimes in harsh light, sometimes in soft shadow. They may be lit from above or below, depending on where they are sitting or standing. A crush of bright garments, carpeting, and upholstery absorbs, reflects, and ultimately changes the light. The artist's challenge was to depict people's skin, clothing, and other objects accordingly to capture the truest possible colors of the scene.

When the house lights went down and the show began, other types of illumination took over. Light flooded the stage in various ways depending on the mood required by the production. Dramatic or subdued, colorful or austere, these effects captured the Impressionists' eyes and ended up being portrayed in their work.

A remarkable example of this approach can be seen in Edgar Degas's paintings of ballerinas in performance. Footlights shine upon the dancers from the edge of the stage, casting shadows back and upward. Degas captures the angle and intensity of the light perfectly as it falls on people, clothing, and objects. The result is

In *La Balançoire* Renoir deftly captures the interplay of light and shadow. The dappled light is central to the painting, particularly as it highlights the young woman in the white dress.

distinctly theatrical—brilliant in front but darkened to the rear. In these paintings, Degas evokes the feeling of times and events long past.

A Legacy of Light

The heyday of the Impressionist era was short. The Impressionists' experiments with light, however, had a monumental and lasting impact. As one art historian puts it, "Impressionism, the first bombshell launched against academic tradition, defined light as color, becoming the first modern language of paint. Sun-drenched and spontaneous, these [paintings] invite viewers to consider the ideas and techniques that opened the door to modern visual expression."[24]

The term "modern visual expression" does not describe one specific technique. It covers the entire gamut of paintings created from the Impressionist era to the present. It refers to the fact that since the late 1800s artists have felt increasingly free to express themselves in any and every way they like. People have experimented with every imaginable way to depict the world's many aspects, including its varying light qualities.

These experiments have sometimes gone to extremes. One modern art critic grumbles, "If the Impressionists were ambitious enough to put it on canvas, the painters who succeeded them pressed home their efforts even further." The results sometimes strayed so far from reality that they were, says the same critic, "transformed to the point of being unrecognizable."[25]

With their devotion to capturing true images, the Impressionists might not have agreed with this result. But they undoubtedly would have supported the artist's right to dream and to create. The Impressionists, after all, were rebels in their own time. They would understand better than anyone that when it comes to painting light, experiments can pay off in unexpected and sometimes wonderful ways.

Chapter Four

An Eye on Everyday Life

A visitor strolling through an art gallery in the early to mid-1800s expected to be impressed, and the most renowned artists of the time did not disappoint. They painted massive works with themes of historical, religious, or social importance. Each canvas was painstakingly planned and executed with the goal of commemorating and, the artist hoped, glorifying the subject it portrayed.

Some artists, of course, had simpler aspirations for their work. They painted landscapes, still lifes, their friends, and other things that pleased them personally. Many of these pictures were skillfully done. In the eyes of the art establishment, though, the quality of the work was irrelevant. Because of their inferior subject matter, these paintings were considered mere trifles, produced by dabblers who did not deserve to be considered real artists.

The Impressionist movement was important partly because it challenged this way of thinking. The Impressionists were convinced that everyday life *did* matter and that it *was* worthy of artistic attention. Devoted to this belief, they channeled their talents into portraying the sights and scenes around them. Critics noticed and commented on the change. "The subjects are no longer the same as those in the official galleries: very little mythology or history; contemporary life, especially among the common people," says writer Théophile Thoré in a review of an exhibition that included the Impressionists' work. "Things are as they are, beautiful or ugly, distinguished or ordinary."[26]

Today this type of approach is taken for granted. In the Impressionists' time, though, it was revolutionary. The Impressionists, in essence, turned their backs on the accepted definition of "good" art. In doing so, they managed to prove a lasting point: The ordinary could be extraordinary. These artists turned their eyes onto everyday life, and they turned the art world upside down in the process.

Reinterpreting the Classics

Some aspects of this shift started to occur even before the Impressionist era. Important ground was broken by Édouard Manet in particular with two works completed in 1863. The artist's masterworks of this year, *Dejeuner sur l'herbe* and *Olympia*, were both based on classic paintings by renowned artists. But Manet's versions twisted and, according to viewers, perverted the originals in a decidedly unseemly way.

A look at each painting shows how Manet tweaked conventions to fit his personal vision. In *Dejeuner sur l'herbe* (Luncheon on the Grass), Manet borrows part of a 1515 composition by the Italian engraver Marcantonio Raimondi. Marcantonio's print, entitled *Judgment of Paris*, shows many heroically naked figures rendered in carefully classic style. The image depicts a scene from mythology that had been painted many times by many different artists, and which was considered both important and significant.

In contrast, Manet's painting shows two men and a woman enjoying a picnic in a grassy park. It is a normal scene apart from the fact that the men are fully clothed and the woman is nude. She stares straight at the viewer, relaxed and unashamed, completely casual in her nakedness. In the background, another half-clothed woman rinses her skirt in a stream. It is not clear if this woman is part of the group in the foreground or if she is just passing by. Either way, she is scandalously underdressed for a day at the park.

An even more striking contrast exists between the work *Olympia* and its inspiration, a painting entitled *Venus of Urbino* (1538) by the Italian master Titian. In *Venus of Urbino* a naked goddess reclines on a sumptuous couch. Calm and lovely, she peeks shyly at the viewer from an averted angle. Her carefully draped hand hides her private parts and preserves her modesty.

A Woman's Place

In the mid-1800s a woman's place in society was highly restricted. Respectable young women did not jaunt about with men or visit bars and cafés. They did not wander city streets by themselves. They were expected to restrict themselves to domestic activities, particularly the raising of children and the nurturing of older family members. They could take a few art classes if they wished. But because they were not allowed to attend life drawing classes, where nude models were displayed, they missed an important part of the curriculum.

These constraints had a major impact on the work of Berthe Morisot and Mary Cassatt, the two most important female Impressionists. Morisot and Cassatt were both skilled artists with partial formal educations. Due to their sex, however, their social options and therefore their subject choices were very limited. As a result, Morisot and Cassatt focused more on domestic images than their male colleagues did.

This focus had a fascinating outcome. For the first time, skilled female artists were tackling stereotypically female subjects such as baby care and bathing rituals. Morisot and Cassatt captured these scenes from a woman's perspective, injecting a warmth and intimacy into their paintings that few male artists could match. Cassatt in particular is known for her tender domestic portraits. She painted many scenes of women, babies, and children, always communicating the closeness of the mother/child bond. Like the works of the male Impressionists, these paintings broke new ground in their unusual yet impactful focus on the everyday.

In *Olympia* Manet closely copies Titian's composition. Instead of a gentle goddess, however, the central figure in Manet's work is a brazen prostitute. The girl's nude body is realistic, not idealized, and her pose suggests a complete lack of self-consciousness. She stares frankly at the viewer, her gaze part challenging, part bored, as if she is taking a well-earned rest between visitors.

Manet's choice of subject matter and his unacceptable departure from tradition caused a scandal when *Dejeuner sur l'herbe* and *Olympia* were first shown in 1863 and 1865, respectively. Critics complained loudly about every aspect of both paintings. A few viewers, however, found originality and honesty in Manet's approach. "When our artists give us Venuses, they correct nature, they lie," points out Émile Zola. "Édouard Manet asked himself why lie, why not tell the truth: he introduced us to Olympia, this [girl] of our time, whom you meet on the sidewalks."[27] Zola, at least, found something to like in this groundbreaking work.

Landscapes

Much less controversial but still revolutionary in their own way were the many landscapes painted by the Impressionists. This trend was significant because before the Impressionists' time, landscapes were considered boring and unimportant. Talented artists did not waste their time on such trivial matters. By embracing this somewhat lost art, the Impressionists greatly boosted its popularity and acceptance.

The Impressionists were not the first French artists to rediscover landscape painting. The École des Beaux Arts had offered a landscape prize to its students since the early 1800s, and some independent painters were also devoted to landscape art. One artist in particular, Jean-Baptiste-Camille Corot, was gaining notice for his gentle landscapes in the late 1820s. By the 1830s Corot's work had inspired a group, later dubbed the Barbizon School, to take up landscape painting.

This movement greatly influenced the young Impressionists, who all dabbled in landscape painting to some extent. Following in the footsteps of their friend and mentor, Camille Pissarro, they differed from the Barbizon School by working solely outdoors rather than in the studio. Along with this change, Pissarro also encouraged his friends and his students to apply the characteristic Impressionist techniques to the task of landscape art. "Work at the same time upon sky, water, branches, ground, keeping everything going on an equal basis and unceasingly rework until you have got it," he once explained to a student. "Paint generously and unhesitatingly, for it is best not to lose the first impression."[28]

No one took this advice to heart more than Alfred Sisley. For Sisley, landscape painting was a lifetime obsession. This Impressionist painted almost nothing other than the natural world, and he loved to capture his favorite places on canvas. He was particularly drawn to the French country towns just outside of Paris, where he painted hundreds of scenes showing the area's rivers, forests, and skies. Thanks to this body of work, Sisley is remembered as one of the Impressionists' premier landscape artists.

Close-Up on Nature

The Impressionists' interest in nature was not confined to landscape painting. These artists also enjoyed the details of the natural world. They sometimes narrowed their focus to capture specific objects of interest.

The best-known example in all of Impressionist painting is undoubtedly Claude Monet's *Water Lilies* series. All of the more than 250 works in this collection were painted in Monet's garden in Giverny, France, during the last thirty years of the artist's life. They depict the sun-dappled, lily-dotted surface of the garden's pond from different angles and perspectives. Portraying the same subject over and over, yet endlessly varied, these works proved the potential of close-up work.

> **Words in Context**
> *floral*
> A painting that depicts flowers, either in vases or in nature.

Magnificent florals, or paintings of flowers, offer another a good example of this approach. All of the Impressionists produced some floral paintings, but of the group, Pierre-Auguste Renoir is probably best known for this type of work. Renoir painted canvas upon canvas of vases

The Impressionists also experimented with still-life subjects, as can be seen in *Still Life with Flowers and Fruit* by Monet. Still lifes provided a different way to explore color and light; they also brought in badly needed income.

exploding with bouquets of freshly cut flowers. In most of the paintings, the flowers come in every imaginable shape, size, and color. They are not artfully arranged. Rather, they are all jumbled together, as if they had just been plucked from a garden and bunched together—

which, indeed, they usually were. When painting flowers, as with anything else, Renoir and the other Impressionists always sought to capture the moment.

Along with florals, the Impressionists also tried their hands at still-life work. A still life is a painting that depicts a carefully arranged, nonmoving assortment of objects. In general, this type of work was not overly interesting to the Impressionists, who preferred to paint moving, modern, open-air images. But still-life work did provide an opportunity to experiment with color, light, and painting techniques. For this reason—and also because still lifes sold well—the Impressionists produced a good number of these paintings.

The Impressionists' close-up paintings were important mostly because of the way they were executed. They displayed the same choppy, unfinished brushstrokes the Impressionists used for their outdoor works. They used broken color and complementary colors for effect and contrast. They also served as experiments in lighting. A bouquet sitting in a sun-drenched room, for example, looked much different than one in a dimmer environment.

> **Words in Context**
> *still life*
> A painting that depicts mostly nonliving subject matter, usually arranged to create a desired effect.

The Impressionists strove to capture these differences in their characteristic style. In doing so they proved that less detail could sometimes create a greater impact, and in the process they changed the way the art world thought about some traditional genres.

City Life

The Impressionists may have been fascinated by nature, but it is important to remember that they were all city dwellers—at least in the early years when they all met. The Impressionist movement was launched in the heart of Paris, a bustling urban center that offered endless sights to delight the artistic eye. With their typical zest for capturing the everyday, the Impressionists enthusiastically painted many aspects of city life.

Some of the most famous paintings of this type were produced by Gustave Caillebotte. Although Caillebotte was part of the Impressionist group and exhibited in their shows, his painting style was traditional and his works were carefully composed, very much in the old-school style. But Caillebotte betrayed his modern leanings in his subject matter. Baron Haussmann's new, glittering Paris was one of this artist's favorite subjects.

Caillebotte's signature work in this regard is a piece entitled *Paris, a Rainy Day* (1876–1877). The large painting shows a city intersection on a gray, drizzly day. Somberly dressed men and women bustle to and fro, protecting themselves from the weather with dark umbrellas. No particular event or item of importance catches the viewer's eye. The scene merely shows Paris, plain and simple, in an image that one author calls "one of the most arresting Impressionist images of modern life—both a celebration and a critique of the brutal, dehumanizing geometry of Haussmann's urban plan."[29]

Smaller in scope but just as urban in tone were Monet's paintings of the Gare Saint-Lazare, one of Baron Haussmann's new railway stations. The stations were something completely new, unprecedented in previous ages. As such, they made fascinating subjects. Monet was particularly mesmerized by the way steam and smoke rose from the trains, swirling and collecting beneath the Gare's high roof, and he painted this effect from many different angles. To get the exact look he wanted, the artist even pestered the station master for special treatment. "The trains were all halted; the platforms were cleared; the engines crammed with coal so as to give out all the smoke Monet desired,"[30] the artist's son recalled years later.

The Social Scene

The rebuilding of Paris did not result only in urban vistas. It also created social opportunities for its residents. Young and carefree during the heyday of the Impressionist era, Parisian art students were very much a part of this social scene. As usual, they were eager to paint the things they saw and did—and according to at least one critic of the time, they did it very well. "The Impressionists show

Gustave Caillebotte was among the Impressionists who favored scenes of city life. In *Paris, a Rainy Day*, Caillebotte depicts a typical city scene—somberly dressed men and women sheltering from the rain beneath black umbrellas.

their particular talent and attain the summit of their art when they paint our French Sundays . . . kisses in the sun, picnics, complete rest, not a thought about work, unashamed relaxation,"[31] writes critic René Gimpel.

Of all the Impressionists, Renoir was the most devoted practitioner of this genre. Renoir was a happy man who loved the social whirl and his friends. He also loved to paint people enjoying themselves. These traits led to a large body of work celebrating the fun side of Paris.

One such work entitled *The Luncheon of the Boating Party* (1881) has been described as "perhaps the most successful celebration of friendship, summertime, and joie de vivre in all of art."[32] The painting shows a group of young men and women enjoying food and

Monet's Garden

After Claude Monet's death in 1926 the artist's house and gardens in Giverny, France, suffered through decades of neglect. By the mid-1900s the once splendid property had fallen into extreme disrepair.

This state of affairs lasted until 1966, when an organization called the Académie des Beaux-Arts took ownership of the historic property. The Académie planned an ambitious repair and remodeling project that began in 1977. Ten years and much hard work later, the house and gardens had been restored to their former magnificence.

Today Monet's house and garden operate as a tourist attraction. More than half a million people visit the property each year to stroll through the gardens portrayed in some of Monet's best-known works. The most popular destination is the water garden, where visitors can enjoy flowers planted by Monet himself or stroll over Monet's famous Japanese bridge. They can even sketch or paint the scenery if they like. In this way today's artists can follow in the brushstrokes of history's most famous Impressionist.

wine at the Restaurant Fournaise, one of Renoir's favorite haunts. The friends are completely relaxed, happy, and maybe just a little bit tipsy. The scene is bathed in the warm light of the afternoon, which dances on the diners' skin and on the bottles, glasses, and fruit on the table.

On the surface, there is nothing extraordinary about this scene. It is something that might happen anywhere along the Seine on a pleasant afternoon. But in typical Impressionist style, Renoir manages to find something special in this very ordinary moment. The painting's subjects are obviously delighted with each other and with the day. Through his exuberant brushwork, Renoir not only captures but clearly shares this feeling, thereby elevating the ordinary to the extraordinary.

Harsh Realities

Life was not merely a series of pleasant picnics for Parisians, of course. Even the happiest people had their dull moments and their troubles. And Paris itself had a dark side, too, as all big cities do. The Impressionists wanted to record the truth, so they did not neglect these aspects of their world. They painted some depressing and even squalid scenes of modern urban life.

An often cited example of this subject matter is *L'Absinthe* (1876), a painting by Edgar Degas. The central figure of this work is a shabbily dressed woman sitting in a public bar. The woman looks unbearably bored, depressed, or perhaps both, and the empty absinthe bottle next to her hints that she may be more than a little bit drunk on this highly alcoholic beverage. She ignores the last full glass of the characteristically green-tinted alcohol that sits on the table in front of her and sits still, staring vacantly into the distance. Her expression and posture give an impression of utter hopelessness and disappointment with a life gone wrong. It is a seedy scene, and one that would never have been painted by the grand artistic masters of old—but there is no denying the painting's power. Degas recognized this fact when he chose his subject, and he did a masterful job of bringing the moment to life.

Words in Context
portrait
A painting that depicts a person or several people as its main subject.

A subtler example of the Impressionists' harsh realism can be seen in the group's family portraits. Instead of painting happy, perfect, idealized families, as previous artists had done, many of the Impressionists painted what they truly saw—and what they saw was sometimes disturbing.

Degas's masterpiece entitled *The Bellelli Family* (1860) embodies this uncompromising approach to portraiture. The piece is displayed today at the Musée d'Orsay in Paris, France. The museum's catalog sums up the painting with these hard-hitting words: "This portrait evokes the family tensions isolating each member of the family. The imposing dimensions, the sober colours, the structured games of open perspectives (doors and mirrors), all converge in strengthening a climate of oppression. . . . The almost playful position of the younger daughter alone, crossing her leg under her skirt, contrasts with the heavy atmosphere whereas her elder sister seems already prisoner of adult conventions."[33]

Portraying this type of dysfunctional undercurrent was unheard of in its time, and it is even more surprising when one considers that Degas was related to the Bellelli family. Art historians question whether Degas really intended to produce such a raw painting of his own relatives. The tension in the image, they feel, may have been the unintended result of long artistic habit. Degas always recorded what he saw, and in this case the artist observed more than he or his subjects had bargained for.

Everyday Moments

L'Absinthe and *The Bellelli Family* are two examples of Impressionist work that seem to tell hidden stories. In this respect these paintings had ties to the past and its long artistic tradition of storytelling, even though their subjects were decidedly ordinary. In general, though, the Impressionists had little need for narrative. They were perfectly content to paint fleeting moments that had no special meaning or weight.

Pissarro devoted much of his life to this type of work. Pissarro was not very interested in well-to-do city residents and their idle amusements. Rather, he was fascinated by the rural fields outside of Paris and particularly by the peasants who toiled there. He painted this population over and over in

Words in Context

narrative

When applied to paintings, a work's attempt to tell a story as implied by the elements included in the piece.

Artist Camille Pissaro applies Impressionist techniques to *A Shepherd at Montfoucault, Sunset*. Pissaro preferred to paint outdoors in natural settings over working in a studio.

the most ordinary moments imaginable. A glance at Pissarro's catalog shows, for instance, washerwomen with their hands buried deep in soap suds, housemaids chatting near a well, farmhands taking a lunch break, and countless other everyday scenes.

Pissarro's scenes were notable, in part, precisely because they *were* so ordinary. They did not try to tell any stories. They simply recorded things exactly the way they were. In a book about the artist, author and art historian John Rewald comments on this matter-of-fact approach. "Rather than glorifying—consciously or not—the rugged existence of the peasants, [Pissarro] placed them without any 'pose' in their habitual surroundings, thus becoming an objective chronicler of one of the many facets of contemporary life,"[34] he says.

While Pissarro chronicled country life, other Impressionists turned their eyes to the city. Paintings of Parisian hot spots have more hustle and bustle than Pissarro's simple rural scenes. Still, many famous works display the same interest in the everyday. An example is Manet's work entitled *A Bar at the Folies-Bergère* (1881–1882), the central image of which is a bored bartender waiting for her next customer. A large mirror behind the woman reflects a large, festive throng of theatergoers in front of the bar. The bartender is not watching the crowd, though. She is daydreaming, waiting, calmly and capably ready to perform her duties. In this image, Manet manages to find the extraordinary in the ordinary—a complete turnaround from traditional thinking.

Friends and Family

When considering the question of ordinary versus extraordinary, nothing is less remarkable than a person's family and close friends. Most artists of the day would not have considered these people to be worthy subjects. The Impressionists, however, took a keen artistic interest in everything around them, and the people in their closest circles were no exception. These artists painted their spouses, their children, their extended family, their friends, and even themselves whenever inspiration struck. These intimate scenes are now considered a defining characteristic of Impressionist art.

> **Words in Context**
> *realism*
> In art, the attempt to paint subjects truthfully, without artificial or unbelievable elements.

This pursuit was important for both artistic and historic reasons. In an artistic sense, the Impressionists' paintings of friends and family broke new ground by popularizing a previously ignored topic. These works were executed with the Impressionists' typical attention to light, color, shadow, composition, and other elements. They clearly showed that any subject, no matter how mundane, could be the basis for exceptional art.

The historic impact of the Impressionists' personal paintings was less immediate. In the long run, though, it would prove to be just as important. Because they were friends as well as colleagues, the Impressionists spent a lot of time in each other's company. They worked together and played together. They visited each other's homes and went on group expeditions. Many of them stayed in close contact as the decades went by. They watched the others raise families and get older. They painted portraits of each other throughout this long stretch of time. In doing so, they chronicled a fascinating period in art history.

The Impressionists had no idea that they would become so famous when they painted these pieces, and they had no sense of creating a permanent record. They were simply enjoying themselves and following their artistic whims. It is lucky that they did. The Impressionists' portraits of friends and family have allowed this amazing group to live on in the minds and hearts of art lovers everywhere. Remembered personally as well as professionally, the Impressionists now embody a particular brand of talent, determination, and courage that inspired many artists of the past—and continues to inspire artists in the present.

Source Notes

Introduction: What Is Impressionist Art?

1. Louis Leroy, "L'Exposition des Impressionists," *Charivari*, April 25, 1874, in John Rewald, *The History of Impressionism*, rev. ed. New York: Museum of Modern Art, 1961, pp. 318–24.
2. Quoted in Andrew Forge and Robert Gordon, *Monet*. New York: Abrams, 1989, p. 58.

Chapter One: Setting the Scene

3. Pierre-Auguste Renoir, letter of March 1881, in Richard Frie-denthal, *Letters of the Great Artists: From Blake to Pollock*, trans. Daphne Woodward. New York: Random House, 1963.
4. Quoted in P. Mantz, "Exposition du Boulevard des Italiens," *Gazette des Beaux-Arts*, April 1, 1863, in George Heard Hamilton, *Manet and His Critics*. New York: WW Norton, 1969, p. 41.
5. Shelley Rice, *Parisian Views*. Boston: MIT Press, 1997, p. 9.
6. Michael Howard, *Encyclopedia of Impressionism*. London: Carlton, 1997, p. 171.
7. Quoted in Diane Kelder, *The Great Book of French Impressionism*. New York: Artabras, 1997, p. 69.

Chapter Two: Tools and Techniques

8. Quoted in Encyclopedia.com: World Eras, "Claude Monet," 2003. www.encyclopedia.com.
9. Howard, *Encyclopedia of Impressionism*, p. 197.
10. Ernest Chesneau, "Le Plein Air, Exposition du Boulevard des Capucines," *Paris-Journal*, May 7, 1874. http://Artchive.com.
11. Kelder, *The Great Book of French Impressionism*, p. 69.
12. Leroy, "L'Exposition des Impressionists," pp. 318–24.

13. M.E. Chevreul, *The Principles of Harmony and Contrast of Colours, and Their Applications to the Arts*, trans. Charles Martel. London: Henry G. Bohn, York Street, Covent Garden, 1860, p. 11.
14. Chevreul, *The Principles of Harmony and Contrast of Colours, and Their Applications to the Arts*, p. xliv.
15. Eugène Delacroix, *The Journal of Eugène Delacroix*, trans. Walter Pack. New York: Supplement, 1937, p. 730.
16. David Kadavy, "Design for Hackers: Why Monet Never Used Black, & Why You Shouldn't Either," *Kadavy.net* (blog), September 28, 2010. http://kadavy.net.

Chapter Three: Capturing the Light
17. Quoted in Kelder, *The Great Book of French Impressionism*, p. 107.
18. Quoted in Rewald, *The History of Impressionism*, p. 369.
19. Quoted in Gerd Muesham, trans., *French Painters and Paintings from the Fourteenth Century to Post Impressionism: A Library of Art Criticism*. New York: Ungar, 1970, p. 497.
20. Quoted in Kelder, *The Great Book of French Impressionism*, p. 111.
21. Quoted in Impressionist Art Gallery, "Haystacks, at the End of Summer," Impressionist Art Gallery. www.impressionist-art -gallery.com.
22. Quoted in A. Cauderlier, "Grainstack Haystack Series," Claude Monet Life and Art. www.intermonet.com.
23. Kelder, *The Great Book of French Impressionism*, p. 206.
24. Greenville County Museum of Art, "Legacy of Impressionism: Languages of Light," 2014. gcma.org.
25. Quoted in *Art Encyclopedia*, "Legacy of Monet's Impressionism." www.visual-arts-cork.com.

Chapter Four: An Eye on Everyday Life
26. Théophile Thoré, review of the Salon des Réfusés, posted on Donatienne: Espace Artistique, April 24, 2012. http://donatien netheytaz.blogspot.com.
27. Quoted in Frits Andersen, "The Scandal of Realism," in Karen-Margarethe Simonsen, Marianne Ping Huang, and Mads Rosendahl Thomsen, eds., *Reinventions of the Novel: Histories and Aesthetics of a Protean Genre*. Amsterdam: Rodopi, 2004, p. 79.

28. Quoted in John Rewald, *The History of Impressionism*. New York: Abrams, 1990, p. 458.
29. Jude Welton, *Impressionism*. London: Dorling Kindersley, 1993, p. 30.
30. Quoted in Howard, *Encyclopedia of Impressionism*, p. 169.
31. Quoted in Impressionist Art Gallery, "Renoir Boating Party." http://impressionist-art-gallery.com.
32. Kelder, *The Great Book of French Impressionism*, p. 208.
33. Musée d'Orsay, "Edgar Degas: The Bellelli Family." www.musee -orsay.fr.
34. John Rewald, *Camille Pissarro*. New York: Abrams, 1989, p. 20.

For Further Research

Books

Phillip Dennis Cate, Daniel Charles, and Christopher Lloyd, *Impressionists on the Water*. New York: Skira Rizzoli, 2013.

Jill Devonyar and Richard Kendall, *Degas and the Ballet: Picturing Movement*. London: Royal Academy Books, 2011.

Simon Kelly, April M. Watson, and Nelson-Atkins Museum of Art, *Impressionist France: Visions of Nation from Le Gray to Monet*. Saint Louis, MO: Saint Louis Art Museum, 2013.

Michael Marmor and James Ravin, *The Artist's Eyes*. New York: Harry N. Abrams, 2009.

James H. Rubin, *How to Read Impressionism: Ways of Looking*. New York: Harry N. Abrams, 2013.

Ann Temkin and Nora Lawrence, *Claude Monet: Water Lilies*. MOMA Artist Series. New York: Museum of Modern Art, 2009.

Barbara Ehrlich White, *Renoir: His Life, Art, and Letters*. New York: Harry N. Abrams, 2010.

Websites

Brain Bashers (www.brainbashers.com). This site has an extensive selection of optical illusions, including many that involve complementary colors.

Color Matters (www.colormatters.com). This celebration of color theory examines many aspects of light and color in an easy-to-understand way.

Fondation Claude Monet (http://fondation-monet.com/en/). The official website of Claude Monet's Giverny home provides background on the artist plus information about how to visit Monet's former home, now a favorite tourist attraction.

Impressionism: Art of Impressionists (www.impressionism.org). This website includes basic information on practically every aspect of the Impressionist movement. It covers technique, participants, history, image galleries, and more.

The Metropolitan Museum of Art (www.metmuseum.org). On this site visitors can search the Met's catalog of holdings to view 372 famous Impressionist works.

Pierre-August Renoir: The Complete Works (www.pierre-august-renoir.org). This site has compiled images of nearly eighteen hundred Renoir paintings. It includes a biography of the artist.

Index

Picture Credits

Kris Hirschmann has written nearly three hundred books for children. She owns and runs a business that provides a variety of writing and editorial services. She lives near Orlando, Florida, with her husband, Michael, and her daughters, Nikki and Erika.